MW01492287

Backing Up

in

Windows 10

Never lose data again,
using tools you already have
and tools you get for free

An *Ask Leo!* Book

1st Edition

by

Leo A. Notenboom

https://askleo.com

Copyright © 2018

PDF: 978-1-937018-46-7
Paper: 978-1-937018-48-1

CONTENTS

The Ask Leo! Manifesto

I believe personal technology is essential to humanity's future.

It has amazing potential to empower individuals,
but it can also frustrate and intimidate.

I want to make technology work for you.

I want to replace that *frustration* and *intimidation*
with the *amazement* and *wonder* that I feel every day.

I want it to be a *resource* rather than a *roadblock*;
a *valuable tool,* instead of a source of *irritation*.

I want personal technology to empower you,
so you can be a part of that amazing future.

That's why *Ask Leo!* exists.

Leo A. Notenboom
https://askleo.com

First: A Freebie for You

Before we dive in, I have something for you: a copy of ***The Ask Leo! Guide to Staying Safe on the Internet – FREE Edition***. This ebook will help you identify the most important steps you can take to keep your computer and yourself safe as you navigate today's digital landscape.

It's yours free when you subscribe to my weekly *Ask Leo!* newsletter.

Each week, you'll find fixes to common problems, tips to keep your computer and online information safe and secure, commentary on technology issues of the day, and even the occasional explanation as to just why things are the way they are. It's educational and fun, and can help you be more effective, more confident, and less frustrated as you use technology.

And it's completely FREE.

Visit https://go.askleo.com/news101 to learn more, browse the archives, and sign up, today!

Be Sure to Register Your Book!

Your purchase of this book entitles you to several additional free bonuses.
- All available digital formats of the book as direct downloads. Regardless of which version you purchase, you can enjoy this book on the digital device of your choice.
- Digital updates for life.
- Errata and prioritized Q&A.

You'll find the information you need to register in a chapter near the end of the book. Once you register, you'll be taken to a web page that lists all available bonuses.

INTRODUCTION

I'm sure you're aware by now that I'm a huge fan of backing up.

Microsoft Windows includes several tools that, used together, can provide a suitable backup strategy to protect you from most of the things that can go wrong.

Let's review what it means to use those tools together properly and get you backed up. We'll also review the impact of Microsoft's decision to phase out one of those tools.

1. Make an image

Start by making an image backup of your computer. It doesn't matter if you don't know what to do with it—that'll come later. By creating an image of your computer, you'll have a known point to which you can always return should anything go wrong in the future.

Creating a Backup Image Using Windows' Built-in Backup walks through the steps to create a complete image backup of your machine on an external hard drive, using what Windows 10 calls the "Windows 7" backup and restore tool.

2. Make a recovery disk

Next, I recommend making a Windows recovery disk. This is a disk (a DVD or USB thumb drive) from which you would boot your machine to restore the image you took in the first step. The Windows recovery disk also includes additional tools to examine and possibly repair your system, as well as the ability to reinstall Windows 10 from scratch if needed.

Create a Windows 10 Recovery Drive walks through the process of creating a recovery drive. You may also want to review the article How do I boot from CD/DVD/USB in Windows 8 & 10? and test to make sure you can boot successfully from the recovery drive you've created.

3. Restoring an image

Restoring an image is the process of taking a backup image you've previously created and putting it back on your computer's hard drive (which erases anything currently on that hard drive). An image restore is exactly what you would do after replacing a faulty hard drive with a new, empty one.

Restoring an Image Backup Using Windows 10's Built-In Backup uses the image we took in step 1 and the recovery drive created in step 2, and walks through the process of restoring that image to your computer.

4. Restoring files from an image

I rely on image backups primarily because there's no question about what's in them: everything. But sometimes you don't want to restore everything; you just want a single file, folder, or collection. Microsoft doesn't make it obvious, but you can do that with a backup image you create using the Windows backup tool.

Restore Individual Files from a Windows Image Backup shows you how.

5. Set up File History

With image backups under our belt, we can move on to more silent, "in the background" backing up in the form of File History. File History sets aside some amount of space on your hard disk—ideally an external hard disk, and possibly the same one containing your backup images—to which it writes copies of your data files each time they are changed. Using File History, you can recover a file as it was an hour ago, a week ago, or sometime in between, depending on how often files change and how much space you've set aside for it.

Enable File History in Windows 10 tells you how to set it all up.

6. Restore a File using File History

After you've had File History running for a while, you'll surely encounter a point where you want to recover a file that has been backed up.

Restoring Files with File History show you how to browse what's been backed up, locate the file or files you want, and restore them.

7. Use OneDrive for Backup

Backing up to a completely different physical location—often called "offsite" backup—has never been easier with the advent of cloud storage and synchronization tools like OneDrive.

Using OneDrive for Nearly Continuous Backup shows you not only how to set up and configure OneDrive itself, but also discusses a couple of simple changes to your workflow that result in almost continuous cloud backup of all your work in progress.

8. Restore a file from OneDrive history

Just like File History, the day will come when you need to recover a file that's been backed up to the cloud.

Recover Deleted Files in OneDrive points out that OneDrive has a Recycle Bin from which you can recover deleted files. As a bonus, Recovering from Ransomware with an Online Backup discusses how it can even save you from ransomware.

⊙

Used together, those eight steps and three tools (image backups, File History, and OneDrive), can provide an adequate level of backup for the average user. Best of all, they're tools you already have in Windows 10.

For now.

Apparently, Microsoft has decided to pull the plug on the "Windows 7 Backup and Restore" tool in Windows 10. It is at least "deprecated," and will likely be removed from a future Windows 10 update. The official word from Microsoft is that you should use third-party utilities instead.

The following bonus four steps do exactly that: show you how to perform the same tasks using the *free* edition of EaseUS Todo, instead of Windows' own image backup tool.

⊙

9. Make an Image using EaseUS Todo

Creating a Backup Image Using EaseUS Todo Free shows you how to create an image backup of your system to your external hard disk.

10. Make a recovery disk for EaseUS Todo

Creating an EaseUS Todo Emergency Disk walks you through the process of creating a recovery disk—what EaseUS calls an "emergency disk"—that can be used to restore an EaseUS Todo image. It won't have the additional tools that the Windows recovery disk created in step 2 had, so you may want both, but you'll need an EaseUS emergency disk to be able to restore images created by EaseUS Todo.

11. Restore an image using EaseUS Todo

Restoring an Image Using EaseUS Todo shows you how to restore a backup image created by EaseUS Todo to your hard disk, replacing everything on it.

12. Restore an individual file from an image using EaseUS Todo

Restoring a File from an EaseUS Todo Image Backup: EaseUS Todo makes restoring individual files and folders from an image backup easy, and this article walks you through the process.

⊙

Backing up is important. I say it so often because it's so true.

I also say it because I see so much data loss, and accompanying heartbreak, because people don't realize just *how* important it is until it's too late.

You can use the steps above to make sure you're appropriately backed up and never suffer data loss again.

CREATE A BACKUP IMAGE

It's no secret that I'm not a huge fan of the image backup software built into Windows. To my thinking, it's too obscure, too inflexible, and doesn't do a good job about telling you what's going on.

It does, however, have a couple of very strong positive attributes: it's free and already on your machine.

And it'll do what I consider to be the bare minimum.

Since the bare minimum is much, much better than nothing, let's create an image backup using Windows Backup.

Windows image backup

The instructions and examples below all use Windows 10, but as we'll see, the backup program has been the same since Windows 7.

In Windows 10, click on the Start button and start typing "backup". One of the first search results should be "Backup settings". Click on **Backup settings** to open the settings app.

Click on **Go to Backup and Restore (Windows 7).** This will open Control Panel on the old Backup and Restore tool. If you're running Windows 7, you can find this directly in Control Panel.

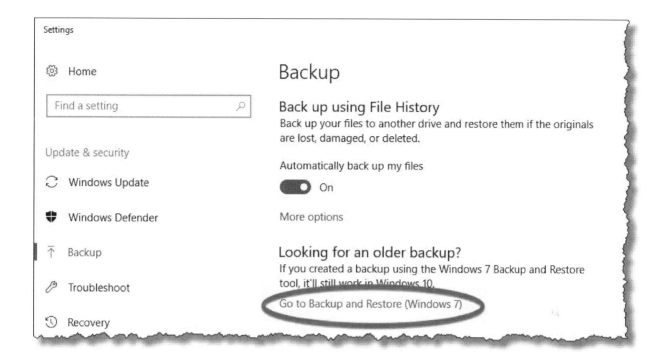

Creating an image backup

Click on the **Create a system image** link on the left.

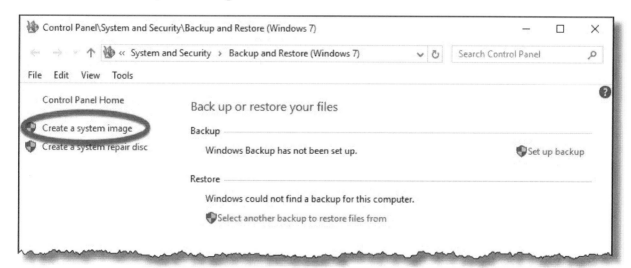

You'll be asked where you want to place the backup.

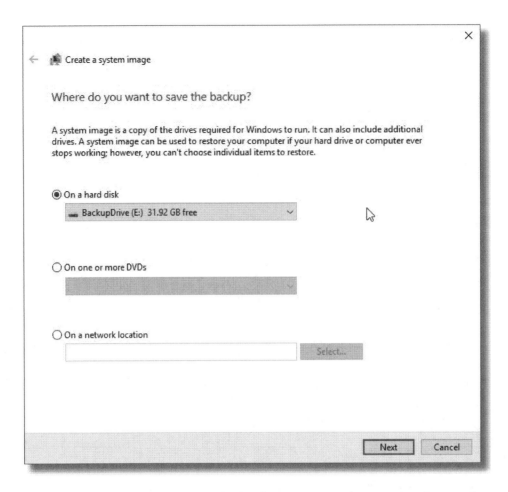

Naturally, you'll need someplace to put the backup image you're creating. I strongly recommend using an external hard disk with plenty of free space. DVDs tend to be impractical, since so many would be required. Network locations are an option, but beyond the scope of this article.

Once you've selected the external hard drive to use, click **Next**. You'll be presented with a summary of what's about to take place. Click **Start backup**.

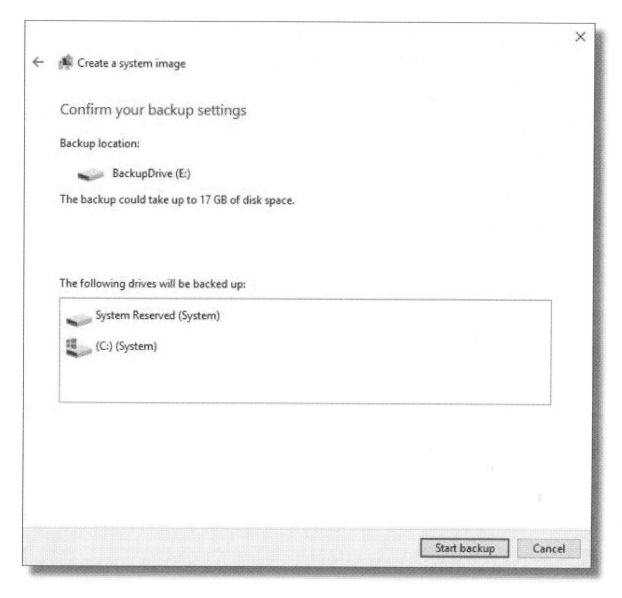

The backup will take some time.

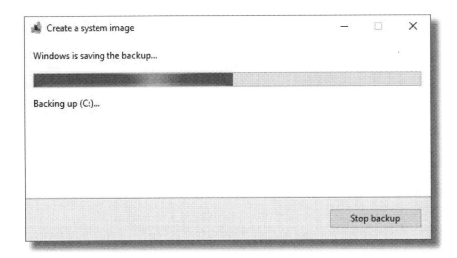

How much time, I can't say, since it depends on the speed of your system, the speed of your hard disks, and how much data is being backed up. You can continue to use your system while the backup proceeds, if you like.

Eventually, the backup completes. When it completes, you'll be asked if you want to create a system repair disc.

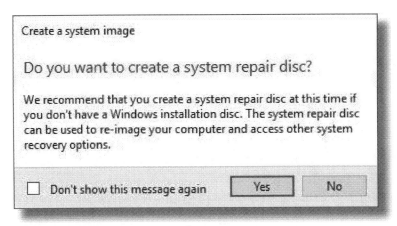

A system repair disk is used to restore system images to your computer, particularly if your computer can't boot normally. If you have your original Windows installation media, you don't need a system repair disk.

Congratulations! You have a system image backup.

MAKE A RECOVERY DISK

A recovery drive is a USB flash drive from which you can boot your computer in order to restore a previously created image, as well as perform a number of other Windows recovery tasks.

You don't have to be taking a backup image to create a recovery drive, and it's actually convenient to have around; it can take the place of your original installation media should that not be available.

Creating a recovery drive

Click on the **Start menu** (or type the Windows key on your keyboard) and begin typing "recovery drive" (without the quotes). The first search result should be "Create a recovery drive". As soon as that appears, click on it.

After giving the **User Account Control** dialog permission to continue, be presented with the Recovery Drive wizard's first screen.

Make sure that "Back up system files to the recovery drive" is checked. This may require a larger flash drive, but ensures you'll be able to reinstall your system from scratch using this drive, should the need arise.

Click **Next**.

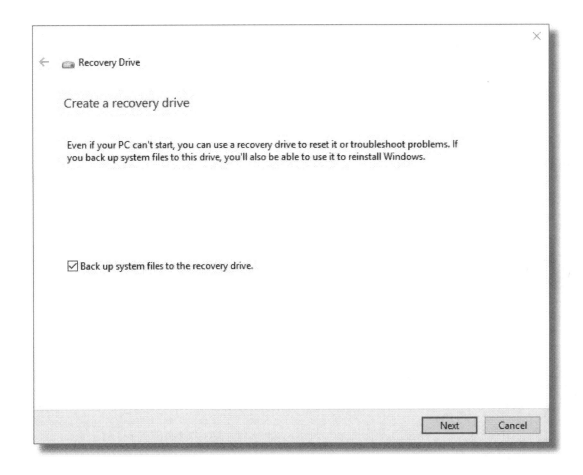

The wizard will scan your system for eligible USB flash drives. If you have not yet inserted a USB flash drive for this purpose, you can do so now, while it scans. The scan can take some time.

When complete, the wizard displays available drives, as well as the minimum size the drive should be.

If more than one is listed, click on the one you want to use, and then click **Next**.

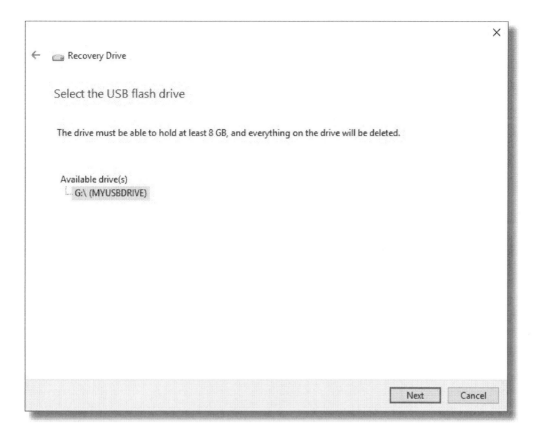

You'll be given an important warning.

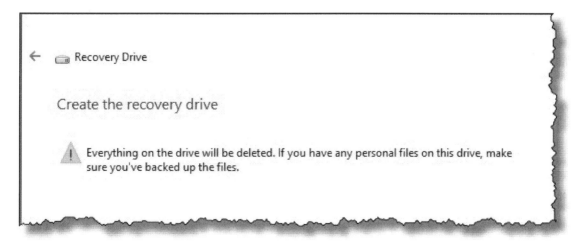

The drive you use for your recovery drive (in this case, my USB drive) *will be completely erased.*

Make sure there is no important data on the drive, and click **Create** to begin the process.

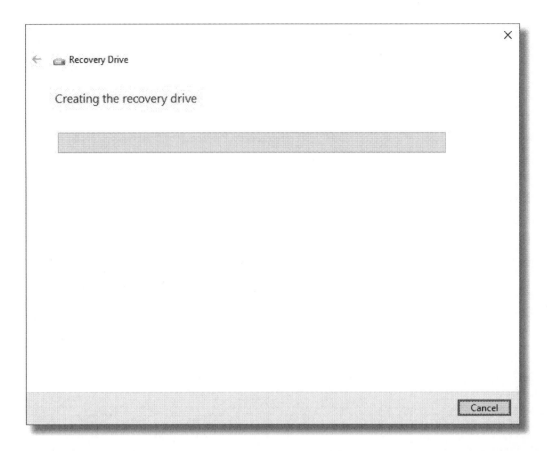

This can take a surprisingly long time—at least it did for me. The length of time depends on the speed of your machine, your flash drive, your USB interface, and even what else you might be doing with your computer as the process proceeds.

When completed, the wizard simply displays a message that it's done.

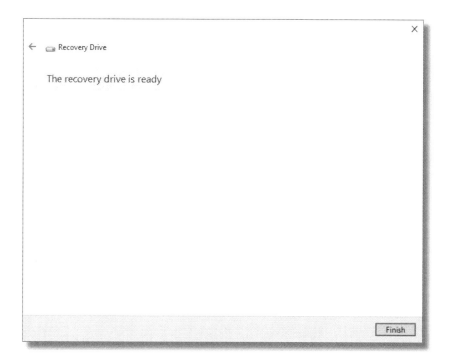

Click **Finish** to exit the wizard.

Using your recovery drive

I'll cover using the recovery drive in more detail later, but the most important thing to realize is that it's something you boot from. By that I mean you reboot your computer, so have your UEFI or BIOS configured to check for bootable USB media before booting normally from the hard disk.

There's more information on exactly what that means in my article How do I boot from CD/DVD/USB in Windows 8 and 10?

RESTORING AN IMAGE

So far, we've taken a system image backup using Windows 10's built-in tools, and we've created a Windows 10 recovery drive we can boot from in order to restore that image.

Now it's time for the rubber to meet the road.

It's time to restore an image backup.

What restoring an image means

Before we begin, it's important to understand exactly what it means to restore an image backup.

Recall that an image backup is a copy of *everything* on your hard disk[1]—the operating system, your installed programs, your data—everything.

The best way to think of an image restore is this:
1. Erase everything currently on the hard drive.
2. Copy the contents of the image to the hard drive.

I can't stress enough the importance of realizing that step one exists. The moment you begin a restore, assume that everything currently on your hard disk is erased. When the restore has completed, everything will be replaced with the contents of the image backup.

That's the whole point of restoring an image backup: replace what's on the hard disk now with what was there when the backup was created.

Step 1: Back up

Ironic as it seems, the first step to consider when restoring is backing up.

Because a restore will remove everything on the hard drive, anything that has been modified or created since the last backup will be lost forever. You may want to save that work first.

There are two approaches:
- Save the specific files and folders that have changed manually, by copying them to another hard disk, flash drive, external drive, or another machine.
- Create an image backup first. This guarantees you've captured everything. We'll be able to extract individual files from it later, should that become necessary.

---

[1] Or one or more partitions on the hard disk, but I'm assuming the images we've created contain all partitions on a given hard disk, backing it up completely.

Of course, there's a third option: do nothing. That's OK, as long as you're aware that any changes since the last backup will be lost.

Step 2: Boot from the recovery drive

Unfortunately, I cannot tell you the exact steps to take to do this. As detailed in How do I boot from CD/DVD/USB in Windows 8 and 10?, the exact steps vary depending on your specific computer.

In general, it involves going into your machine's BIOS or UEFI configuration to change the boot order to look for bootable USB devices before checking the internal hard disk.

Once that change is made, insert the recovery drive made previously (usually a thumb drive), and reboot. When successful, the first screen you'll see will ask you for your keyboard layout.

Step 3: Select the image to restore

After choosing your keyboard layout, you'll be given an option to either "Troubleshoot" or "Turn off your PC". Click on **Troubleshoot**.

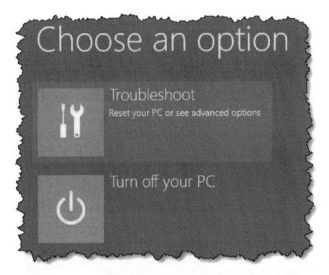

This will give you the option to either "Recover from a drive" or select "Advanced options".

Even though the description for "Recover from a drive" might lead you to believe it's what we want, in reality, this option reinstalls Windows from scratch without restoring your backup. Instead, click on **Advanced Options**.

Click on **System Image Recovery**.

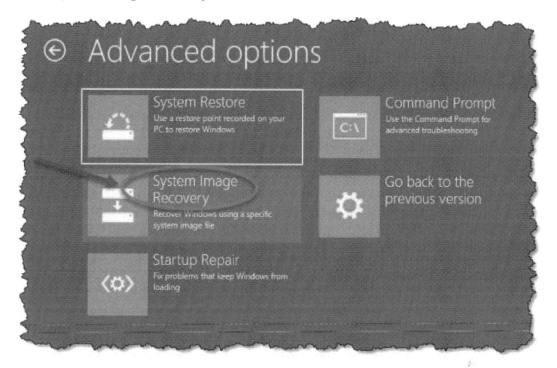

Next, you're asked to "Select a system image backup", suggesting that you "Use the latest available system image".

While that might occasionally be the correct choice, it isn't always. For example, if you took an image backup immediately prior to this, but need to restore to an earlier backup taken before that, you'll want to make sure to select "Select a system image".

Click **Next**.

You'll then be asked to select the location of the backup you want to restore. In the example below, there's only one drive listed, but if you have multiple drives that could potentially contain backup images, click on the drive containing the image you want to restore, and click **Next**.

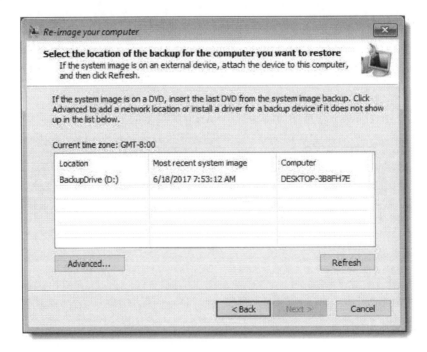

You'll be presented with a list of the backup images contained on the drive you selected, listed by the date and time the image was created. Click on the image you want to restore, and click on **Next**.

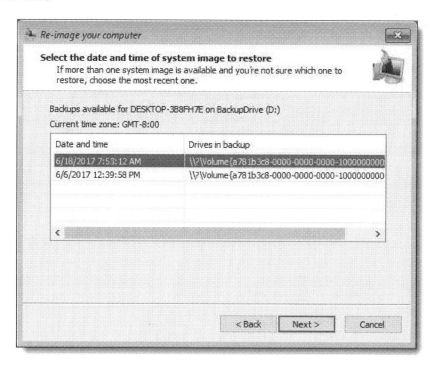

Next, you'll be given the option to "Format and repartition disks". Generally, if you're restoring a backup image to the same hard drive from which it was created, there's no need to do this, and you can leave it unchecked. If, however, you have replaced the hard disk, then check this option to initialize the disk properly prior to the restore.

Click **Next**.

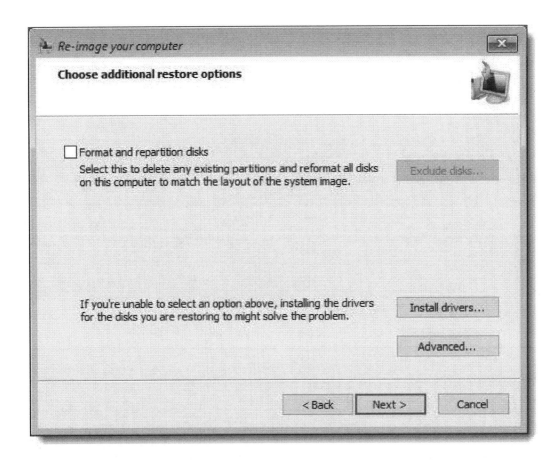

Windows will warn you that everything currently on the hard disk is about to be erased and replaced with the contents of the image. Click **Yes**, assuming that's what you want.

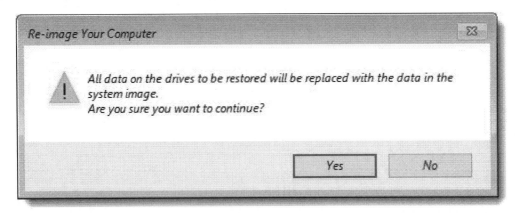

The restore begins.

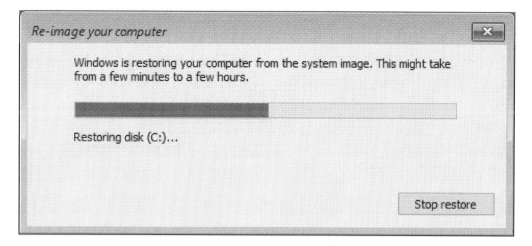

Exactly how long the restore takes depends on the usual things: the speed of your internal and external hard drives, the speed of the interface between them, and the size of the backup image.

Step 4: reboot

Once the restore is complete, it will automatically reboot your computer if you're not around.

If your computer automatically reboots back into the Recovery Drive, simply remove the drive and reboot again.

You've successfully restored a backup image. The system should now reboot into Windows, just as it was at the time the backup image was created.

RESTORING FILES FROM AN IMAGE

To sum up: thus far, we created an image backup using Windows 10's built-in image backup tool, which it refers to as the "Windows 7 Backup." We've also looked at how to restore that image, in its entirety, to your hard disk.

But what if you don't want to restore the entire image? What if all you want is just a single file or set of files contained within the image? That's why image backups are awesome, after all. They contain *everything*.

The good news is you don't need to restore everything if you don't want to.

Let's restore a single file contained within a Windows 10 image backup.

Where's the backup?

The first thing we need to do is to locate the backup. Windows "conveniently" hides all the actual files involved on the backup drive you selected in a single folder called "WindowsImageBackup".

If you examine the contents of that folder (you'll likely be asked to confirm that you want to, and give yourself permission), you'll find a folder with the same name as your machine name.[2]

Viewing the contents of that folder (once again, after confirming your intent) you'll find a series of folders named "Backup", followed by a date and time—one for each image backup stored on the drive. View the contents of the folder corresponding to the date and time of the backup image you want to examine.

Here is where you'll finally find the files you're looking for, though with names that might make no sense to you.

The files we care about—the files that actually contain the image backup—are those with the filename extension ".vhdx". In the "type" column you'll see them described as "Hard Disk Image File".

25fd0423-f036-4c2a-b92b-276e373a73cb_Writer6813297...	6/18/2017 9:01 AM	XML Document
a781b3c8-0000-0000-0000-501f00000000.vhdx	6/27/2017 10:10 AM	Hard Disk Image File
a781b3c8-0000-0000-0000-100000000000.vhdx	6/27/2017 10:10 AM	Hard Disk Image File
BackupSpecs.xml	6/18/2017 9:01 AM	XML Document

---

[2] If you back up multiple machines to the same drive, this keeps the backups for each machine separate.

Choosing the right file

If your backup contains multiple partitions—and most backups do these days— you'll have more than one ".vhdx" file, with names that don't relate to anything you might recognize. Each corresponds to one backed-up partition. In the example above, for example, one is the "System Reserved Partition", and the other is my "C:" drive.

Which is which? We'll use the size of the image to guide us. Looking at the sizes of the two files, you'll see that one is significantly larger than the other.

25fd0423-f036-4c2a-b92b-276e373a73cb_Writere813297…	6/1	5,524 KB
a781b3c8-0000-0000-0000-501f00000000.vhdx	6/2	16,982,016 KB
a781b3c8-0000-0000-0000-100000000000.vhdx	6/2	419,840 KB
BackupSpecs.xml	6/1	2 KB

That tells us that the first one is the larger of the partitions on my hard disk, and contains the backup image of the "C:" drive. Note that this size will not match the actual size of the partition—it contains only data, and may also be compressed—but the relative size of the files should correspond to the relative size of your partitions. Reserved or recovery partitions are almost always significantly smaller than the data partitions of a hard disk.

This technique is quick and easy, but it doesn't always work. If you have multiple partitions containing roughly the same amount of data, their backup images may be roughly the same size. In these cases, it's easiest to simply pick one and examine its contents, as we're about to do. If it's the wrong one, repeat the process with the other.[3]

Mounting the hard disk image

Right-click on the image file containing the image you want to examine, and click on **Mount**.

---

[3] There are probably other ways to determine which partition is which in cases like this, including understanding something about the filenames, or examining the contents of other files. Honestly, just looking inside is probably the easiest and will take about the same amount of time.

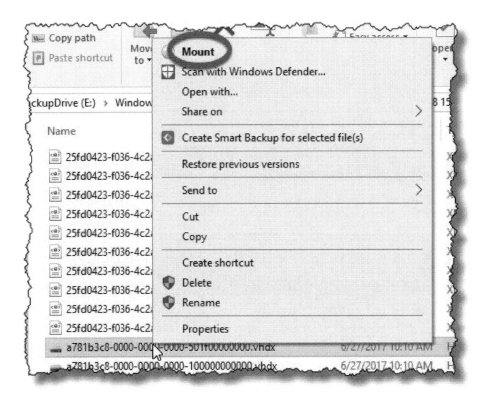

This instructs Windows to take that image file and treat it as if it were an actual hard disk.

You may get a warning.

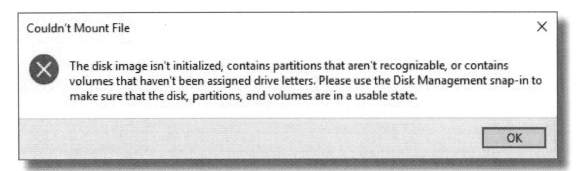

In our case, the warning simply indicates that the drive we're interested in has not yet been assigned a drive letter—normally a part of the mounting process. The instructions it provides to proceed are correct: we'll need to run the Disk Management tool.

Assigning a drive letter

In Windows 10, right-click on the **Start** menu and click on **Disk Management** (or, in any version of Windows, simply run "diskmgmt.msc").

You may need to scroll down within the resulting display, but you should find a large disk partition that has no drive letter.

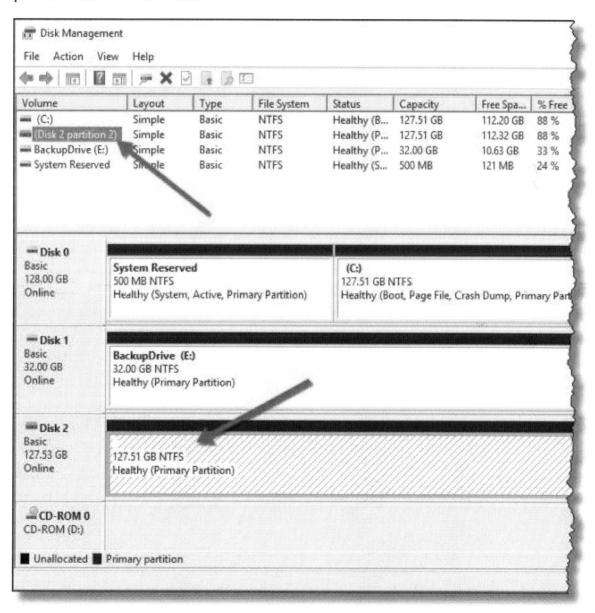

The "Capacity" listed should match the capacity of the partition you backed up, and the free space should roughly match the free space on the drive at the time it was backed up.

Right-click on the disk in the lower pane, and click on **Change Drive Letter and Paths**... in the resulting pop-up menu (not shown). The next dialog will present a list of currently-assigned drive letters and paths showing empty ones, as none have been assigned yet.

Change Drive Letter and Paths for 130570 MB NTFS Simple Vol... ✕

Allow access to this volume by using the following drive letter and paths:

| Add... | Change... | Remove |

OK   Cancel

Click the **Add...** button.

The next dialog will give you a choice to add a drive letter or a path. Make sure "Assign the following drive letter" is selected. Next to that is a drop-down list of drive letters not currently being used by your system. You can select a different letter if you like, or simply accept the default—"F:" in the example below.

Add Drive Letter or Path ✕

Add a new drive letter or path for 130570 MB NTFS Simple Vol....

◉ Assign the following drive letter: F ∨

○ Mount in the following empty NTFS folder:

Browse...

OK   Cancel

Click OK.

Your backup image is now mounted as drive F: on your system.

Examining the image

The reason for going through this lengthy process of locating, mounting, and assigning a drive letter should hopefully now be clear: all you need to do is use whatever tool you like to examine the contents of your backup image. For example, I've opened up drive "F:" in Windows File Explorer below.

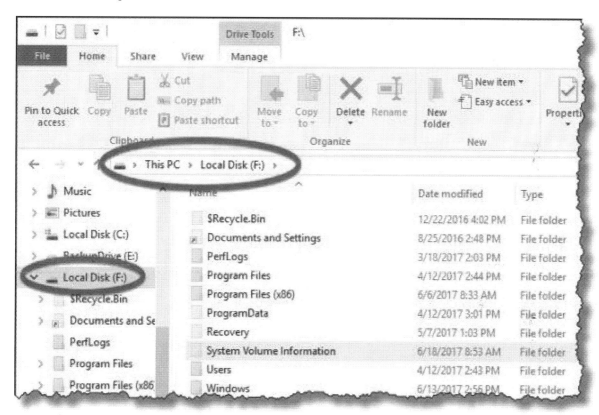

The contents of my "F:" drive look almost exactly like my "C:" drive, which makes sense, since what we mounted was a backup image of the C: drive. (If the contents don't look like the contents of the drive you expect, make sure you selected the correct ".vhdx" file earlier.)

Restoring individual files or folders is simple: just locate them within the mounted image partition—drive F: in my example above—and use whatever technique you're comfortable with to copy them back to your C: drive. That's all there is to it.

Since people often ask: you shouldn't be able to modify the contents of a mounted image. Even if you could, you shouldn't, as it would no longer be an image of the drive when the backup was taken; it would be an image "plus random changes", which in the long term can get confusing.

When you're done

When you're done restoring images from the backup, you need to unmount the drive.

Return to Disk Management, right-click on the disk, and click on **Detach VHD**.

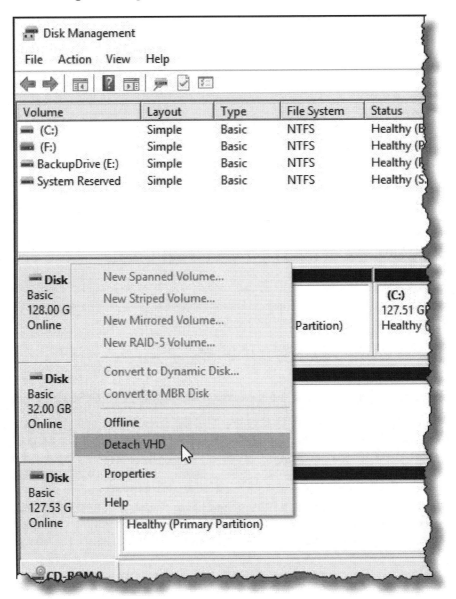

You may be asked to confirm (not shown), after which the mounted drive will disappear.

SET UP FILE HISTORY

Backing up the files you care about on a regular basis is a common (if incomplete) approach to backing up. While I much prefer an image backup, choosing to regularly back up only the files you work on is what many would consider a minimal approach to backing up.

On the other hand, regularly backing up the files you're working on, *in addition to* perhaps less-frequent image backups, represents a more robust back-up strategy.

As it turns out, Windows includes such a feature, and it's called "File History".

Let's build that more robust backup strategy by enabling File History.

What File History does

In concept, File History is a simple feature: every so often, it looks for files that have changed since the last time it looked, and makes a backup copy of any that have.

Those copies are saved to a drive you specify—typically an external drive. In fact, it's quite common to have the same external drive be used for image backups as well as File History.

You can configure File History to remove older backup copies to make room for new ones. The more room you have, the longer backup copies can be kept.

What File History doesn't do

File History is not a replacement for an image backup, because it doesn't back up every file on your machine. It only monitors the contents of specific folders for changes. For example, your "Documents" folder would generally be backed up by File History, but Windows itself, as well as other programs you've installed, are not.

This is why I consider File History a useful *addition* to a periodic image backup, not a replacement.

You might take regularly scheduled image backups once a night or once a week, augmented by File History looking for changes in data files every 10 minutes. Taken *together*, this provides a significant level of protection.

Enabling File History

Click on the Start button, and start typing "File History". Click on **Backup settings** when it appears in the search results.

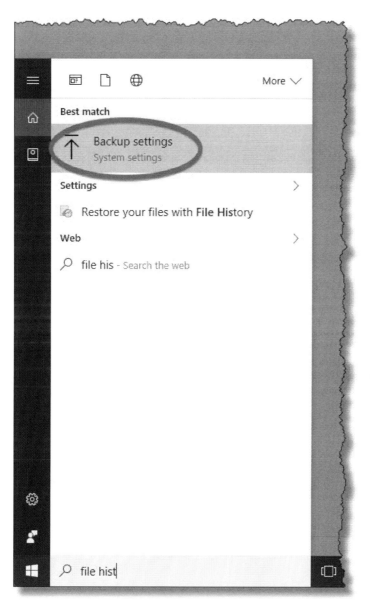

This will take you to the "Back up using File History" page in the Settings app. Click on **Add a drive**.

You'll be presented with a drop-down list of all drives that could be used for File History. Click on the drive you want to use; I strongly recommend an external backup drive.

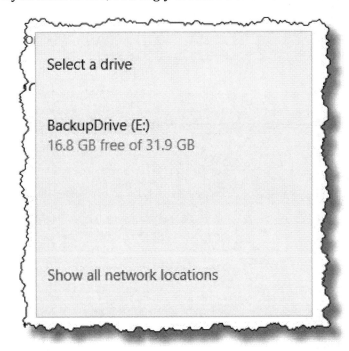

This will replace the "Add a drive" option with the "Automatically back up my files" option turned on.

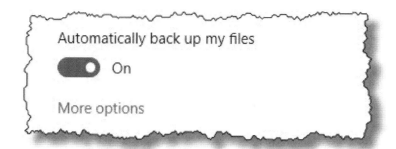

Configuring File History

Click on **More options**. The resulting "Backup options" page has several items of interest.

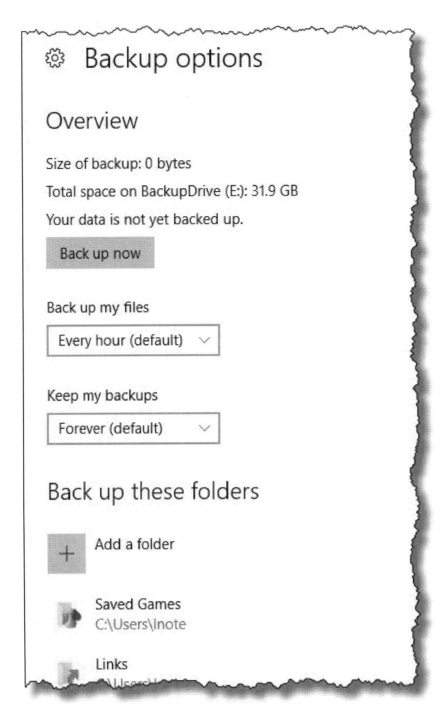

The Overview section provides information on the space used and available, as well as the option to "Back up now".

The "Back up my files" dropdown controls how often File History looks for updated files. The default is every hour, but options range from every 10 minutes to once a day. The more often you back up, the more space will be used, and older backups will be deleted to make room. An hour is a fine place to start.

"Keep my backups" controls how long your backup files will be kept available. For reasons I don't comprehend, the default appears to be "Forever", which almost guarantees that your backup drive will fill up, at which point you'll receive an error message and File History will stop. Click on the dropdown; you'll be presented with a list of alternatives between one month and two years, as well as "Until space is needed". I much prefer the latter as more pragmatic, guaranteeing you'll always have backups of your most recent work.

"Back up these folders" is the list of folders that File History monitors for updates. (All files and subfolders within these folders are monitored.) Click on "Add a folder" to add a folder not currently listed. Conversely, click on one of the folders listed, and a "Remove" button will allow you to remove it from File History's scanning.

Even if you make no changes whatsoever, the "Back up these folders" list is worth reviewing so you have a clear understanding of what File History does, and, just as importantly, *does not* include.

RESTORE A FILE USING FILE HISTORY

Since we turned on File History, our computer has been carefully looking for files that have changed since the last time it looked, and making backup copies of any that have changed to our external drive.

Great. So how do we access those backup copies when we need them?

There are two ways. Both are fairly straightforward.

Restoring an old copy of an existing file

Probably the simplest scenario is when you need an older copy of a file that still exists on your hard drive. Perhaps you made changes to it you want to "undo"; perhaps the file was overwritten by something else; it really doesn't matter what happened. What you want is a copy of the file "as it was" at a specific time in the past.

Fortunately, you had File History turned on, and the file you're concerned about was in one of the folders that File History backs up.

Locate the file in Windows File Explorer, right-click on it, and select "Restore previous versions".

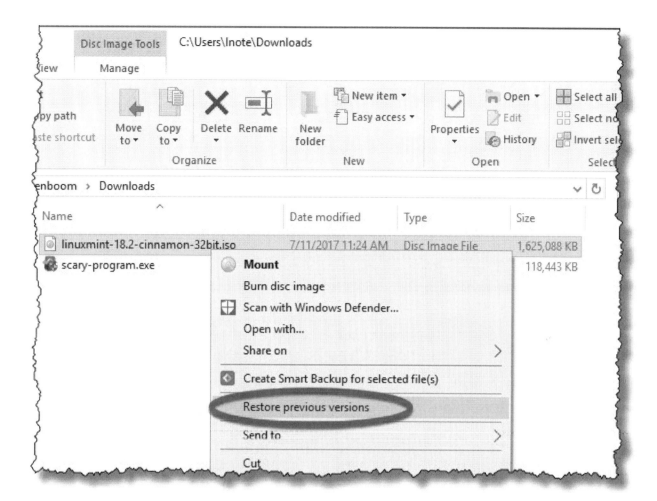

This will open the "Previous Versions" tab of the Properties dialog, listing the current version as well as any previous versions of the file that are available from backup.

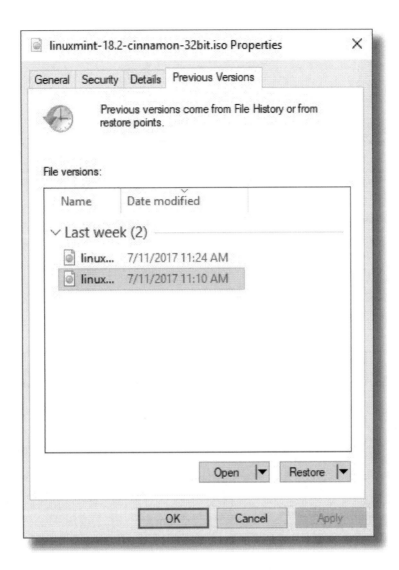

If only one file is listed, and its date and time match the file as it exists on your hard drive, then you have no additional backup copies from which you can restore.

If there are multiple copies listed, select the version of the file you want to restore, and click on the down-arrow next to the Restore button to expose your options.

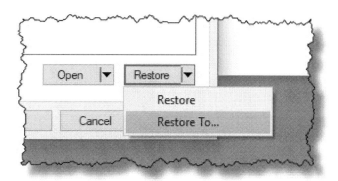

"Restore" replaces the current copy of the file with the backed-up copy, restoring it to the state it was in at the time the backup was created.

"Restore To…" opens a "Save As…" dialog box. This way, you can save the backed-up copy as an additional file, either in a different location or with a different name, without affecting the current copy of the file.

I recommend using one of the Restore options when retrieving a file from File History. The Open button also shown includes two options: opening the file directly from the backup without restoring it, and opening the file in File History, which we'll examine next.

Browsing File History

If the file you want to restore has been
deleted, such that there's nothing to right-click
on in the approach outlined above, or if you
just want to browse around and see what File
History contains, there's an alternate
approach.

Click on the Start menu and type "Restore".
When it appears, click on **Restore your files
with File History**.

This will open the File History browser, where
there are several items of interest.

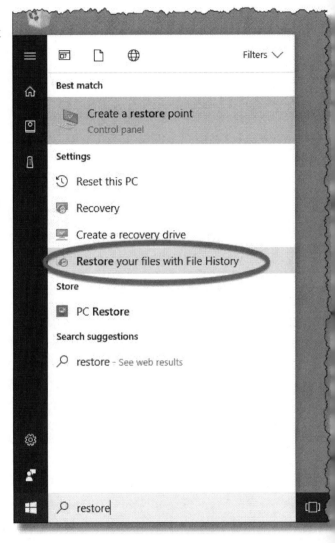

At the top, the browser lists the current folder being examined. "Home", the default location, is the folder located at "C:\Users\<your login name>".

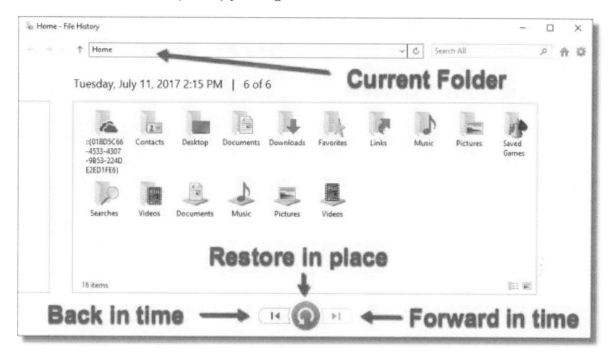

Beneath the current folder is the date and time of the current backup copy being viewed, along with a count of and position within the backups of this folder that are available. In the example above this is the 6th, or most recent "snapshot" of the files, and there are 6 total.

Next is a display, much like Windows File Explorer, of the contents of the folder.

Centered below the file list are three buttons:
- The left-pointing arrow changes the contents displayed to the next most recent backup, moving backward in time.
- The green "restore" button restores the currently selected item back to its original location on your hard drive.
- The right-pointing arrow changes the contents displayed to the next newer backup, moving forward in time.

Using the arrow keys, you can browse through the history of the displayed folder, and use the restore button to restore any file you want to.

To navigate into a folder shown in File History—say the "Downloads" folder, in the example above—simply double-click on it in the file display.

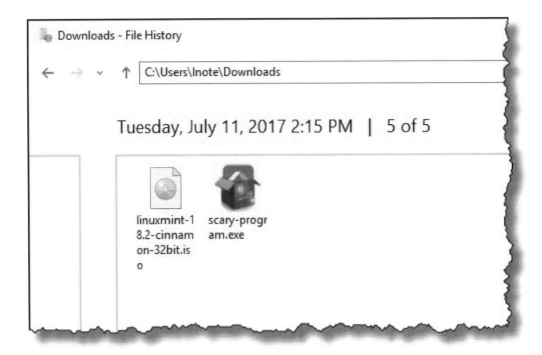

Now you can click the "Back in time" arrow to move into the folder's history. Previously deleted files may appear.

Click on a file you want to restore, click on the green Restore button (labelled as "Restore in place" on the image on the last page), and you'll have recovered the file from File History.

You can continue to navigate through your File History by typing folder locations into the current folder box at the top, if you like, or by clicking on the grey up-arrow to its left to move back "up" in the folder tree, and then clicking on other folders and sub-folders as you like. In each folder, you can navigate through the backed-up File History by clicking the forward-or-backward-in-time arrows.

What File History does and does not back up

It bears repeating that File History is not a substitute for a complete image backup. File History only backs up the contents of specific folders you set; anything outside those folders is not included.

When you set up File History, you control which folders are included, but as we've seen above, even if you were to have it attempt to back up almost everything (not recommended, due to disk space and time) you're limited to restoring individual files or folders only. Restoring your operating system or programs that have been installed via a setup program is simply not what File History is intended for. That's a job for a complete image backup.

USE ONEDRIVE FOR BACKUP

Regularly creating image backups using Windows 10's built-in imaging tool, and setting up File History to back up files that change on a regular basis, is all good.

We can do better.

Best practices for a robust backup strategy call for keeping a backup copy off-site. OneDrive, included as part of Windows 10, can do that automatically.

We'll set up OneDrive and then make a couple of changes to other applications to make our use of OneDrive for backing up nearly transparent.

Microsoft account and connectivity

You need a Microsoft account to use OneDrive.

You may already be using one to log into your PC. If you're logging in with an email address—particularly if it's a @hotmail.com, @outlook.com, @msn.com, or other Microsoft-provided email domain—you already have one.

If not, and you don't have a Microsoft account at all, I'd recommend visiting outlook.com and signing up for a new account. It's free.

You will also need to be online for OneDrive to work. It's best if you're constantly connected, but it'll work with an intermittent connection as well. As with all things online, the faster the connection, the better.

OneDrive

OneDrive is standard in Windows 10. In fact, it's downright difficult to remove. ☺

If OneDrive has not yet been set up, you'll often get a notification to "finish" setting it up, and the taskbar icon may have a red error indicator.

If you don't see the icon, you may need to click the "Show hidden icons" carat (^ – not present above), to find the OneDrive icon in the notification area.

Click the OneDrive icon to launch the set-up process.

Setting up OneDrive

First, you'll be asked for the email address corresponding to your Microsoft account. Type it in and click **Sign in**.

Once signed in, you'll be shown the location of your OneDrive folder (with the option to change that location).

Unless you have a specific reason to change it—such as placing it on a different drive—leaving it at the default location is fine. That location will be "C:\Users\<login id>\OneDrive", where "<login id>" is replaced with your log-in identifier. In the example above, that's "lnote". That puts the OneDrive folder in the same place as your Documents folder ("C:\Users\<login id>\Documents"), your Downloads folder ("C:\Users\<login id>\Downloads"), your Pictures folder ("C:\Users\<login id>\Pictures"), and others.

You'll be presented with a list of folders in your OneDrive account.

Since I already have and use OneDrive, it displays a list of the folders already included there. The contents of all the folders I select will be downloaded and mirrored on my PC. If this is your first use of OneDrive, your folder list may be empty.

Unless you know you have specific requirements otherwise, make sure "Sync all files and folders in OneDrive" is checked. Click on **Next**.

That's it! Well, you may be presented with some "Isn't OneDrive wonderful?" marketing and informational messages, but it's set up. OneDrive is at work.

What OneDrive does for backing up

After setting it up, you might be wondering why we bothered with all that. What's in it for us?

At its most basic, OneDrive operates similarly to other cloud storage services: what's on your hard drive is a mirror—a copy—of what's in your OneDrive account online.

Great. What's that mean?

Two things:
1. Any time you add or update a file or folder within the OneDrive folder on your machine, it is automatically uploaded to OneDrive online.
2. Any time a file appears in OneDrive online, it's automatically downloaded to the OneDrive folder on your machine.

The file is available in both locations, and you can use either.

For our purposes today, that's it. In fact, I'm going to completely ignore the second one and focus entirely on the first: whenever you add or change something in the OneDrive folder on your machine, it's automatically uploaded.

Automatically uploaded.

Or to put another way: it's automatically backed up to the cloud.

Leveraging OneDrive transparently

The easiest way to make sure OneDrive is always backing up your work is to always do your work in OneDrive.

That means instead of creating your new documents (or Pictures, or Music, or whatever) in your "Documents" folder, create them in your OneDrive folder. Then, every time you hit "Save", the document is updated on your disk and uploaded to your OneDrive online account.

Put another way, every time you hit "Save", your document is backed up to the cloud. Your PC could be destroyed, but your document(s) will still be there, online, in your OneDrive account.

The easiest way to do this is to change the default folder your applications use. Unfortunately, that's not a global setting; it's something you need to locate and change for each application.

Some applications remember the last folder you used and automatically use that folder the next time you create or save a document. Others will not remember at all, and you need to remember to Save your document to your OneDrive folder. Others, like Microsoft Word (shown below), have options buried in advanced settings that allow you to change the default location.

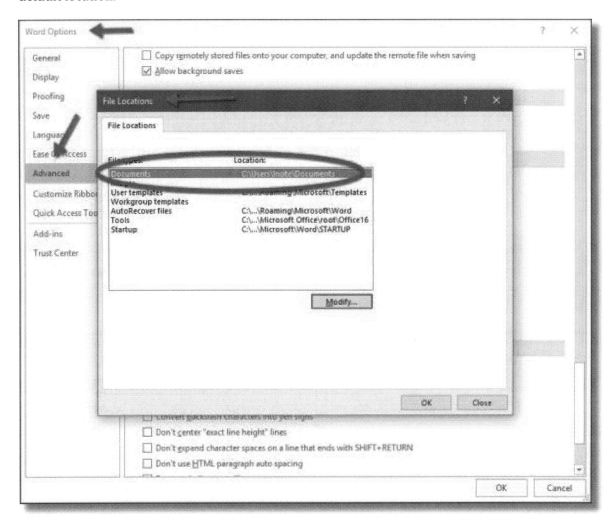

The default will almost certainly be "C:\Users\<login id>\Documents". You want to modify that to be "C:\Users\<login id>\OneDrive". If you're like me, and like to keep things organized, you might create a folder within your OneDrive folder—perhaps "WordDocs"—and set the default location to "C:\Users\<login id>\OneDrive\WordDocs". Now all the new documents you create will:

- Be created in OneDrive.
- Be automatically uploaded every time you click on "Save" or exit the program.

It may seem like a little hassle to locate the options within the programs you use most often, but it's something you need to do only once …

… and it'll pay off any time you need to grab a file from your OneDrive online backup.

RESTORE A FILE FROM ONEDRIVE HISTORY

You've deleted some files on your computer, and you've emptied the Recycle Bin.

Now you wish you hadn't deleted that one important file. Whoops.

On top of that, you did all this a few days ago, so data recovery tools are unlikely to work.

If you've been doing your work within your OneDrive folder, however, there is hope.

OneDrive's Recycle Bin

Did you know OneDrive has a Recycle Bin of its own? For the longest time, I didn't. It wasn't until the scenario I outlined above actually happened to me[4] that I found it out of desperation.

OneDrive's Recycle Bin works just like the Recycle Bin on your PC: when you delete a file in your OneDrive folder, it's not really deleted, but instead moved to your OneDrive Recycle Bin.

OneDrive's Recycle Bin is completely separate from the one on your computer, and has different rules about how long it keeps things. Your computer's Recycle Bin permanently deletes older files to make room when it fills up. The OneDrive Recycle Bin permanently deletes files after 30 days.

How to use the OneDrive Recycle Bin

For this example, I'll start with four files in a OneDrive folder.

---

[4] Fortunately, given my propensity to back up early and often, my reliance on OneDrive turned out to be a convenience—but it can be *very* convenient. Depending on your own backup strategy, it can be downright life-saving.

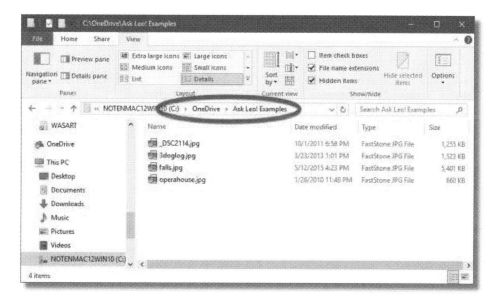

Those files are on my computer, in a subfolder of my OneDrive folder called "C:\OneDrive\Ask Leo! Examples". Since they're in my OneDrive folder, they've also automatically been uploaded to my online OneDrive account.

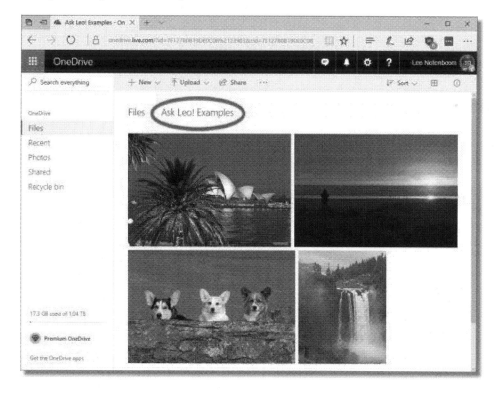

You can view the contents of your own OneDrive Recycle Bin by clicking on the **Recycle bin** item on the left-hand menu in OneDrive online. (For clarity, my OneDrive Recycle Bin is empty.)

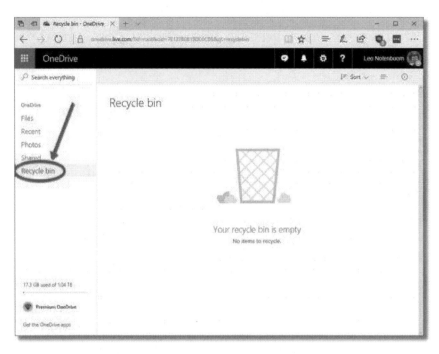

On my computer, I delete one of the files. Within a few seconds (or minutes, depending on your internet connection), that deletion is mirrored to OneDrive online, and I'm left with only three files in both locations.

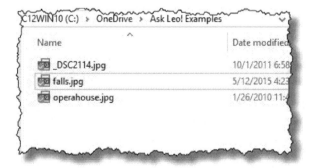

Restoring a recycled file

In OneDrive online, click on that **Recycle bin** link in the left-hand menu to view a list of files deleted in the last 30 days. In my case, that's the file I just deleted. Right-click on the file you want to restore, and click on Restore.

The file will be restored to its previous location in your OneDrive folder online. As soon as your computer's OneDrive app synchronizes (typically in a few seconds or minutes), the file will reappear on your computer as well.

Recycle bin and philosophy

As a matter of safety and general philosophy, you should never count on the Recycle Bin being there.

I say that because I hear from people who purposely place things in their Recycle Bin and are surprised when those things disappear—either through the mechanisms I described earlier, or through explicit Recycle Bin cleaning. The Recycle Bin is not meant as a place to keep things; it's a safety net and nothing more. If you want to keep files, but want them out of your way, create and manage your own folders. Then *you* remain in control.

This applies to the Recycle Bin on your computer as well as the one in OneDrive. They're both good safety nets. Like any safety net, you hope you never need it, and should take action to avoid relying on it.

RECOVERING FROM RANSOMWARE WITH AN ONLINE BACKUP

One of the comments I quickly received on my article "Using OneDrive for Nearly Continuous Backup" was this: "If one should fall victim to hostile file encryption, instantaneous backup to OneDrive presumably would result in those being encrypted too."

In other words, if you're using OneDrive (or Dropbox, or other similar services) to automatically back up files online whenever they change, doesn't that mean that ransomware would cause those backups to automatically be replaced with their encrypted versions?

Yes.

But before you give in to a knee-jerk reaction to avoid online backups completely, consider this: they'll give you more options, not fewer, should ransomware ever strike. In fact, they could save you in ways other backups might not.

Online backup to the rescue

Whenever a file is deleted from your computer in a folder being continuously backed up by OneDrive[5], the following happens:

---

[5] I'll keep referring only to OneDrive, as it's baked in to Windows 10, but most of these concepts apply to DropBox as well. Other services may also include similar features, so if you choose to use something other than DropBox or OneDrive, I encourage you to research the options available. The amount of free storage you get is not necessarily the most important factor in deciding which to use.

- Any prior copy of the file is moved to a Recycle Bin on the OneDrive servers.

Whenever a file changes on your computer in a folder being continuously backed up by OneDrive[6], the following happens:

- The prior copy is moved to the version history for that file. (A kind of recycle bin specifically for that file.)
- The new copy is uploaded.

Yes, <u>OneDrive has a Recycle Bin</u>. *This means OneDrive can save your data from ransomware.*

It works like this:

- You use OneDrive to keep a more-or-less continuous backup of your data online.
- Your machine becomes infected with ransomware of some form, and all your data files are encrypted (and therefore lost to you).
- If you are online, OneDrive dutifully notices that the files have changed, and backs up the now-encrypted files.
- You panic. (Technically, this step is optional, but quite common.)
- You disconnect, clean up, rebuild, or otherwise remove the malware from your machine, but are left with all of your files encrypted.
- You visit OneDrive online, and recover your unencrypted files from its Recycle Bin and each file's version history.
- You vow to never again do whatever it was that allowed the malware infection to happen in the first place.
- Life goes on.

OneDrive just saved your bacon. What's more, everything I've described above all happens without any other form of backup in place.

But of course, you also have other forms of backup—right?

Belt and suspenders and suspenders

The person who originally left the comment continued, "A simple, but probably inefficient, means I use is to weekly make a copy within OneDrive of backed up files."

---

[6] Within 30 days, that is. I'd strongly recommend doing it as soon as you possibly can, just for added safety and reassurance.

This is (almost) *exactly* what I do myself. Every night I make a copy, elsewhere on my machine, of everything in my OneDrive folder, in the form of a compressed archive (like a ".zip" file). Should I ever succumb to ransomware, I can recover my files from that additional backup. I would not make the copy "within OneDrive", however, since ransomware could impact that backup copy as well.

Of course, on top of that, I have my nightly backups running to an external hard drive: monthly full backups with daily incrementals, meaning I can always recover the files "as of" a few days ago. (And in case I happen to run across ransomware that also tries to encrypt backups ... some of those backups are copied elsewhere, effectively "offline" and not directly accessible to my machine.)

It would take a lot for even the nastiest ransomware to cause me to lose any significant number of files.

You don't need to go overboard

You don't need to be as backup-crazy as I am. You can protect yourself with just a few simple steps.

- Use OneDrive for nearly continuous backup of your day-to-day working files.
- Enable File History. File History, though sometimes disabled by more aggressive ransomware, will also let you restore a file to the condition it was in prior to encryption, and can protect files outside of those you keep within OneDrive.
- Take periodic full, and more frequent incremental, image backups of your entire system to protect from almost any type of failure.
- Every so often, take one of those full backup images and copy it to offline storage.

And, honestly, that last one is just to make people panicking about ransomware encrypting their backups happy. That doesn't happen so often that I consider it truly critical, particularly with what we've just discussed about OneDrive's Recycle Bin.

Don't let the worst-case scenario scare you away from reasonable choices

What concerns me most are folks who say they won't use online backups because their files *might* be encrypted by ransomware and the online backup would be useless.

Ransomware is only one type of threat. More importantly, it's not even the most likely threat.

For example, a hard disk failure can be *much* more destructive than ransomware, and is probably much more likely to happen. Even more bluntly: you're more likely to accidentally overwrite or delete a file than you are to personally encounter ransomware.

Even if the Recycle Bin didn't exist, continuous online backups save your files from many threats that *don't* involve invalidating the backup.

The same is true for nightly backups to an <u>always-connected external hard drive</u>. Yes, there's a chance that ransomware could encrypt your backups. There's a higher probability that you'll be glad you had those backups current for a variety of other failures.

Making backups easy, timely, and automatic is more important than fearing one specific—albeit destructive—form of malware.

MAKE AN IMAGE USING EASEUS TODO

Apparently, Microsoft has decided to pull the plug on image backups (known as the "Windows 7 Backup" tool in Windows 10). My current understanding is that it is at least "deprecated", and will likely actually be removed from a future Windows 10 update. This will leave Windows 10 with no built-in image backup capability of its own.

The official word from Microsoft is that third party utilities should be used instead. This doesn't break my heart, as I was never a fan of their tool. I had hoped, however, that they would improve, rather than remove, the facility.

EaseUS Todo is a backup program whose free edition is superior to Windows' built-in tool. I'll show you how to create an image backup using it. The bonus is, this is not limited to Windows 10 at all; as of this writing, the free edition works with Windows XP, Vista, and all versions of 7, 8, and 10.

EaseUS Todo

EaseUS Todo can be downloaded from their website. (As always, I strongly recommend avoiding "download sites" and getting software directly from the manufacturer whenever possible.)

There are three things to note about the download and install.

First, you will *repeatedly* be offered the opportunity to choose their retail product or a trial version of their retail product. These products are not free. They're also not needed for what I'm about to show you. Sometime later, you can return and upgrade to one of their paid offerings if you like. For now, be careful to choose the truly FREE version of EaseUS Todo.

Second, you will be asked for an email address. In a sense, this is the "cost" of the free edition. I have no complaints with EaseUS email, and you can always unsubscribe later. They do frequently offer discount codes for their retail product, so if you think you might be purchasing at some point in the future, it's worth getting on their list.

Finally, like most free software, be on the watch for PUPs. EaseUS does not hide the additional software offered with Todo, but it is selected by default. Be sure to deselect it during the install process.

Creating an image

Run EaseUS Todo, and on its main screen, click on Disk/Partition Backup.

I choose this over "System Backup" or "Smart Backup" because it provides explicit control over the disks and partitions included in the backup image.

On the resulting screen, check the box to the left of the disk that contains your system or C: partition. This will ensure that the entire hard disk that contains your system, including any additional partitions (such as recovery partitions), will be included in your backup.

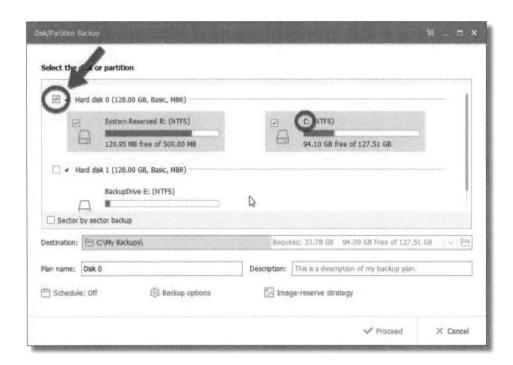

Next, click on the small folder icon to the far right on the "Destination:" line.

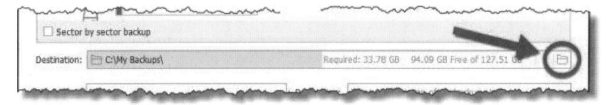

This will open a folder selection dialog box. Use that box to select the destination: the folder, typically on your external hard drive, into which the image backup is to be placed.

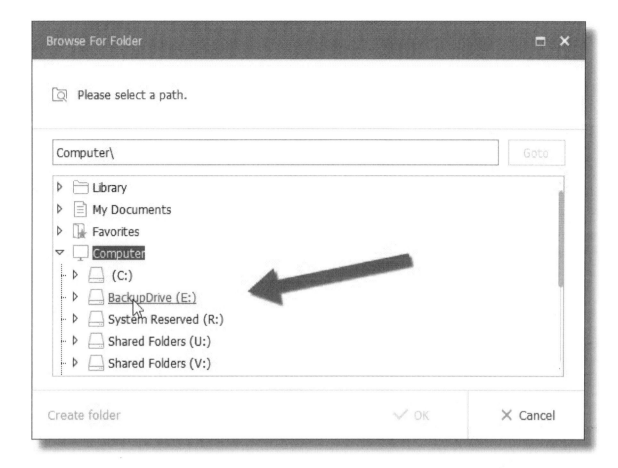

Click **OK** to accept your selected destination folder.

Click **Proceed** to begin the backup.

Naturally, this will take some time. Exactly how long will depend on the speed of your system, the speed of your hard disks, the amount of data to be backed up, and more. I will point out that EaseUS Todo's "Estimated time remaining" indicator is notoriously inaccurate.

Your backup image

Eventually, the backup completes.

Open Windows File Explorer and navigate to your previously selected destination, and you should find a ".pbd" file.

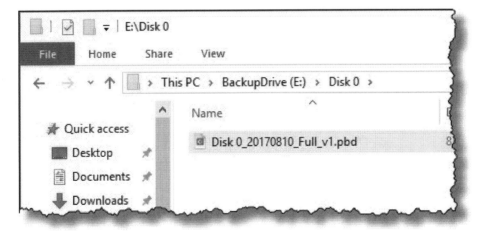

That file contains the image backup of your system.

MAKE A RECOVERY DISK FOR EaseUS Todo

Now that we've created a system image backup using the free version of EaseUS Todo, we need to prepare for the day we might need to restore that image.

It's time to create an "Emergency Disk", as EaseUS calls it.

When and why you need an Emergency Disk

There are two common scenarios that require an emergency disk.

The first is the most obvious: your hard disk fails, and you need to restore your backup to a replacement hard disk. Since that replacement drive is empty, you don't have EaseUS Todo installed to process the recovery. In fact, your machine won't even boot; Windows isn't on that empty hard drive yet!

The second scenario is malware; you want to restore your system to an image backup taken prior to the malware's arrival. You can't boot into Windows, since you wouldn't be able to restore it to its prior state while it's running; you can't overwrite a file while it's being used, and that is especially true if the file is part of the operating system itself.

In both cases, as well as a few others, the solution is to *boot from something else*.

That "something else" is the EaseUS Todo Emergency disk. When you boot from it, it automatically runs a copy of EaseUS Todo you use to locate your backup image and restore that image to your computer's hard drive.

You can create the emergency disk at the time you need it, but only if you have a separate working system on which to do that. More commonly, you'll want to create the disk prior to needing it, while your system is working normally. I'll expand on this below.

Creating an Emergency Disk

Run EaseUS Todo. Click on Tools in the toolbar, and then Create Emergency Disk in the resulting drop-down menu.

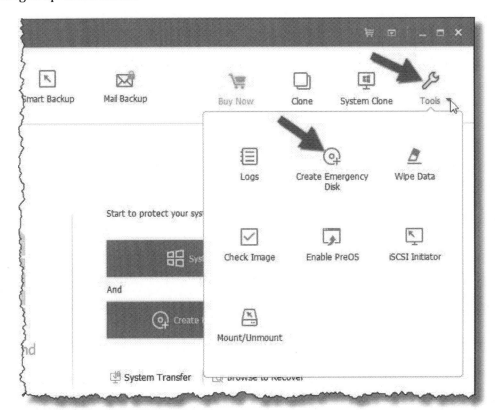

You'll then be shown a dialog box containing several choices.

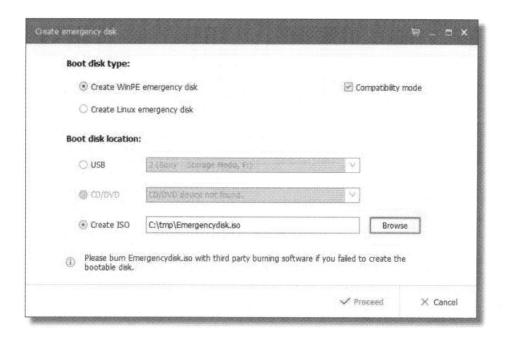

There are two selections to make.

Boot disk type determines whether the Emergency Disk should be based on Windows or Linux. In general, choose Windows (with "Compatibility mode" checked) unless your testing determines that this boot disk doesn't work for some reason, or you've been otherwise instructed by customer support. In general, since your system is already running Windows, the Windows Emergency Disk has the highest probability of just working.

Boot disk location determines what media your disk will be created on.
- Choose **USB** if you have a USB thumb drive you can dedicate to this purpose (it'll be completely erased), and you can configure your machine to boot from USB.
- Choose **CD/DVD** if your machine is capable of burning a CD or DVD, and you can configure your machine to boot from CD.
- Choose **Create ISO** if your machine can boot from CD or DVD, but doesn't have the ability to actually burn a CD or DVD. In this case, you need to specify the location into which an "iso" file will be created. You then take this ISO to another machine that has a CD or DVD burner to actually create the media.

Once you've made selections appropriate to your situation, click on **Proceed**.

After a short period of time, the process completes and the emergency disk is ready.

When to create your emergency disk, or …

There are two schools of thought as to when you need to actually create your Emergency disk.

Create it before you need it. This is important if you have no other computer available from which to make the emergency disk in an actual emergency. You'll need to have it ready to go so you can simply boot from it and deal with whatever the crisis happens to be.

Technically, you should only need to create the emergency disk once. However, there are strong arguments for creating a new one each time EaseUS Todo is updated. I recommend doing so at least for major version updates, to ensure compatibility with the backup software, as well as to address any issues that are updated in the emergency disk itself.

Only create it when you need it. This works if you have another working machine from which to create the emergency disk. The emergency disk does not need to be created on the same machine you've been backing up, or on the machine to which you plan to restore—any Windows PC will do.

If you plan to create it when needed, I do recommend that when that time comes, you download the latest version of EaseUS Todo Free, so as to get the latest version of the emergency disk.

My actual recommendation is that you do both: create one now, test it, and keep it in a safe location in case you need it. Then, when the time comes, you have the option of using that, or, if you can, downloading the latest version and burn a new, more up-to-date emergency disk.

RESTORE AN IMAGE USING EASEUS TODO

Now it's time to use that emergency disk. Let's restore a backup image to our machine.

What an image restore means

It's important to realize exactly what restoring an image means: *it replaces everything on the disk* with the contents of the image.

If you took an image backup on Monday, and it's now Wednesday, restoring Monday's image backup will overwrite everything on the hard disk, and your machine will be as it was at the time of that backup. *Everything that happened on Tuesday and Wednesday would be lost.*

If "what happened" was a malware infection, then that's conceivably exactly what we want. On the other hand, if you did important work on Tuesday and Wednesday you don't want to lose, you'll want to save that work somehow: you could copy the new files elsewhere, or create a new image backup prior to restoring the old one.

Of course, if "what happened" was a hard drive failure and replacement, you may not have a choice. You'll simply restore the most recent image you have.

I'll call it "Step Zero"—prior to performing the restore, if you can, save any data that hasn't been backed up.

Step one: boot from the emergency disk

Unfortunately, exactly how to boot from an emergency disk varies from machine to machine. Check the instructions for your specific computer to learn how to boot from the emergency disk (CD/DVD or USB) you created earlier.

In some cases, it's a simple choice made at boot time.

In other cases, most notably newer machines with UEFI and Secure Boot, the process is more complex.

Locate the image

Booting from the emergency disk automatically runs EaseUS Todo. On its opening screen, click on **Browse to Recover** to begin the restoration process.

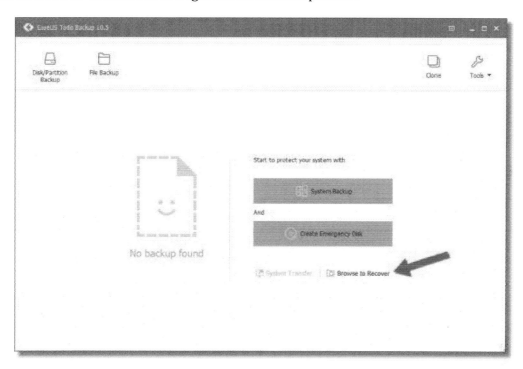

This will open a file-selection dialog box.

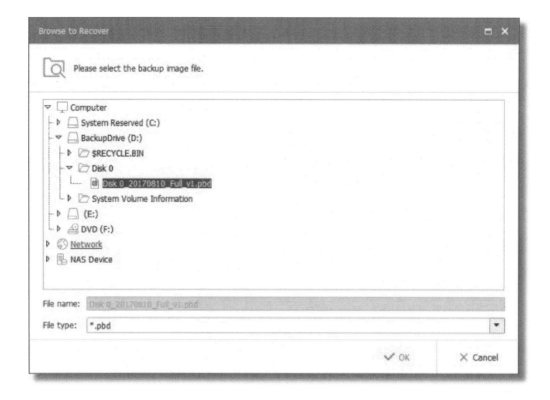

Navigate to the drive and folder that contains your image backup by clicking on the appropriate triangles to the left of each listed item. In the example above, I've navigated through:

- **Computer** – to open the devices available on my computer
- **BackupDrive (D:)** – to open my external drive, which contains the backup image I want
- **Disk 0** – to open the folder containing that image

The file "Disk_0_20170810_full_v1.pbd" is the image file I want to restore. Yours will be named differently, and there may be multiple files. Unless you know otherwise, you generally want the most recent backup image.

It's worth noting that the drive letters you see may be different than what you normally see in Windows. My external drive is normally drive "E:", but when booting from the emergency disk, it appears as drive "D:". This is normal. You'll need to look at the drive's name ("BackupDrive", in my case), and its contents to confirm you're looking at the correct drive.

Once you've selected the appropriate image file to restore, click **OK**.

Next, you'll be shown a dialog displaying the disks and partitions contained within the image you've selected.

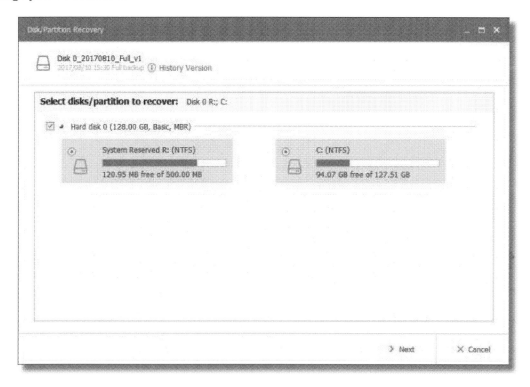

This allows you to choose to restore the entire disk image—by checking the box next to "Hard disk 0", in my example—or unchecking that box and selecting individual partitions within the image instead.

Most commonly, you'll restore the entire hard disk (in the case of a hard disk replacement due to failure, for example), so we'll check the Hard disk box.

Click **Next**.

Select the destination

You'll then be taken to a dialog which displays the drives and partitions to which you might restore your image.

All the hard disks known to your machine will be displayed, possibly including your external drive.

Check the box next to the drive you're restoring to. In our example, that's the first drive listed—Hard disk 0. Once again, note that drive *letters* may be different than what you normally see when running Windows.

Click **Next**. You'll be presented with a summary of what's about to happen.

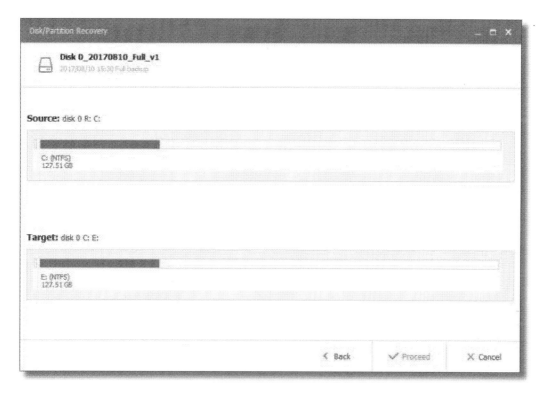

Click **Proceed**.

Remember I said the restore would overwrite everything currently on your hard drive? EaseUS reminds you of that before continuing.

Click **OK**.

The restore begins.

Restore complete

How long the restore takes depends, like the backup, on how fast your drives are, how fast your computer is, and how much data there is to be restored. Progress will be displayed along the way.

Eventually, it finishes.

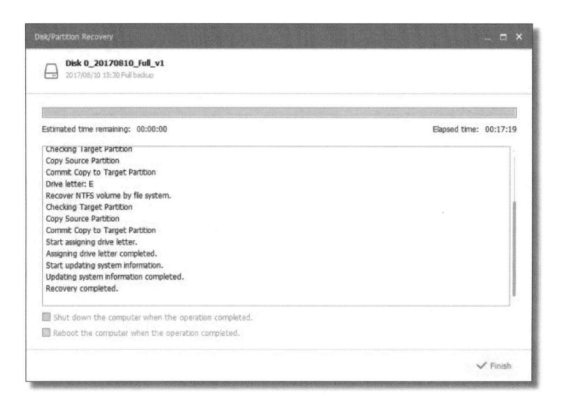

Click on **Finish**, and close EaseUS Todo by clicking on the "x" in its upper right corner.

Your machine will reboot. Take care to remove the emergency disk, or to select your computer's system disk from which to boot. Again, how to do this specifically will depend on your computer.

When the boot completes, you can breathe a sigh of relief as familiar screens appear.

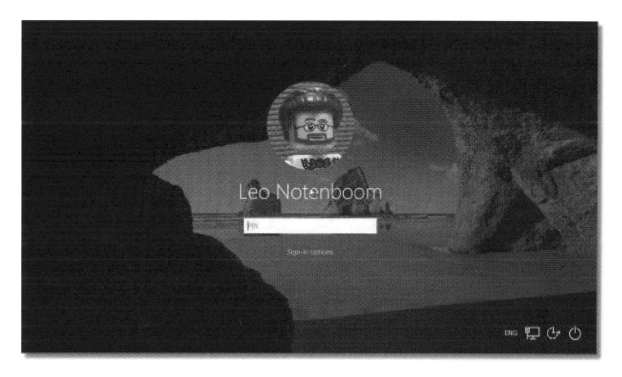

Remember, however: this is Windows *as it was* when you took the backup image.

You've successfully restored your backup image.

RESTORE AN INDIVIDUAL FILE FROM AN IMAGE USING EASEUS TODO

Image backups are one of the most important types of backups, because they backup absolutely everything. Should you need to replace a failed hard drive, for example, an image backup will restore everything and let you continue as if nothing had happened.

But what if you don't want everything? What if you just need a single file you know is somewhere in that image backup?

No problem.

Locate the image

Naturally, you'll need the file or files containing your image backup.

If it's a full backup, then only the single ".pbd" file is necessary. If it's in <u>an incremental backup</u>, you'll need the full image backup it was based on, plus all the intervening incremental backups as well.

The files will be wherever you instructed EaseUS to place them when you created your image backup. Typically, that's on your external backup drive, but it could be almost anywhere with sufficient storage space for your collection of backups.

Navigate to that location in Windows File Explorer.

In the example, above the image file is located in:
- E: – my external backup drive. I told EaseUS Todo to place the image files here when I created my backup.
- Disk 0 – the name of the folder EaseUS Todo created to represent the disk drive it was backing up.

The name of the image file itself—"Disk 0_20170810_Full_v1.pbd"—includes the disk name, the date of the backup, the type of the backup (Full), and the first version of a backup on that date.

If you have multiple files, or if you have incrementals, locate the most recent file so as to access the most recently backed-up files. (If you need to get a file from "a week ago", for example, locate the image file that corresponds to the backup taken immediately after that time.)

Double-click on that file. EaseUS Todo[7] will "<u>mount</u>" the file, making its contents visible within Windows File Explorer.

Navigating the image

Windows File Explorer will open to the top-level contents contained in the image file.

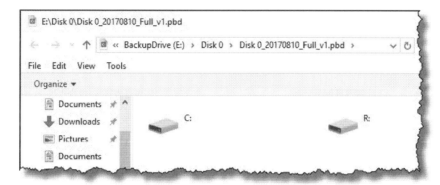

In the example above, the image file contains backups of two drives: "C:" and "R:". Those drive letters were assigned by the system to the two hard drives (or partitions) that were backed up.

Double-click on the drive containing the file(s) you want to restore. In our example, that'll be the original "C:" drive.

---

[7] This all assumes you're working on the same machine you were backing up, and thus have EaseUS Todo installed. You need it installed in order for this process to work.

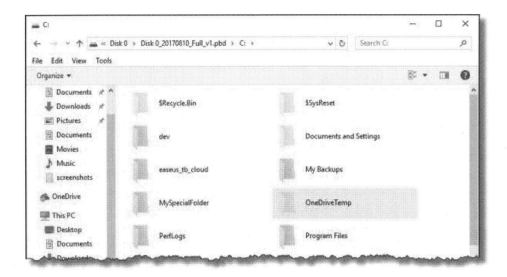

What you'll see is the contents of the <u>root</u> of the C: drive as it was when the backup was taken. You can now navigate through that backup image and examine its contents, using Windows File Explorer just as you would with any other drive.

Restoring your file

Using Windows File Explorer, navigate to your Documents directory within C:. In our example, that's:

- C:
- users
- lnote – (would be replaced with your own login name)
- Documents

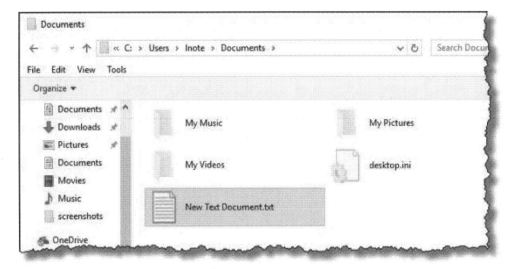

Remember, this isn't the "real" C:; this is all contained within the backup image stored on your external hard drive.

To restore a file—such as the "New Text Document.txt" file in the example above—simply copy it to any folder you like on your actual hard drive—the "real" C:—using any technique you're comfortable with: drag and drop, copy/paste, or something else.

That's all there is to it.

You can repeat this process for as many different files, or even entire folders, as you want to restore from your backup image.

ENDNOTES

Afterword

I hope this book helps you get backed up and protected against all the nasty things that can wipe out your computer's data. It doesn't happen often, but it does happen, and backing up is the best way to protect yourself from any number of different types of disasters.

If it's helped you at all—especially if you're now backed up—I consider this a success.

If you find what you believe to be an error in this book, please register your book (the details are in an upcoming section) and then visit the errata page for this book. That page will list all known errors and corrections, and give you a place to report anything you've found that isn't already listed.

Register Your Book!

Having purchased this book, you're entitled to additional updates, errata, and other bonus materials:

- Updates for life.
- Regardless of how you purchased this book, you can download it in any or all of three digital formats:
  - PDF (for your computer or any device that can view PDF files)
  - .mobi (ideal for the Amazon Kindle), or
  - .epub (for a variety of other electronic reading devices).
- Other bonuses and supplementary material I might make available in the future.

Registering gives you access to it all.

Visit http://go.askleo.com/win10backup *right now* and register.

That link is mentioned *only here,* and it's totally FREE to owners of this book.

About the Author

I've been writing software in various forms since 1976. In over 18 years at Microsoft, I held both managerial and programming roles in a number of groups, ranging from programming languages to Windows Help, Microsoft Money, and Expedia. Since 2003, I've been answering tech questions at the extremely popular *Ask Leo!* website (https://askleo.com) and in entrepreneurial projects like this book.

Curious for more? Someone asked and I answered on the site: Who is Leo? (https://askleo.com/who-is-leo/)

Feedback, Questions, and Contacting Leo

I'd love to hear from you.

Honest.

I truly appreciate reader input, comments, feedback, corrections, and opinions—even when the opinions differ from my own!

Here's how best to contact me:

- If you have a comment or a question about this book, I strongly encourage you to register your book, as outlined in above, and use the prioritized comment form in the registered owner's center.
- If you prefer not to register your book, you can email me at leo@askleo.com.
- If you have a computer or tech-related question, the best approach by far is to first search Ask Leo! (https://askleo.com). Many, many questions are already answered right there, and finding those answers is much faster than waiting for me.
- If you can't find your answer using Search, visit https://askleo.com/book and submit your question. That's a special form just for book purchasers and it gets prioritized attention.
- If you just want to drop me a line, or have something you want to share that isn't covered above, you can use https://askleo.com/book, or email leo@asklco.com.
- If you're just not sure what to do … email leo@askleo.com. ☺

Copyright & Administrivia

This publication is protected under the U.S. Copyright Act of 1974 and all other applicable international, federal, state, and local laws. All rights are reserved.

Please note that much of this publication is based on my own personal experience and anecdotal evidence. Although I've made every reasonable attempt to achieve complete accuracy of the content in this book, I assume no responsibility for errors or omissions. You should use this information as you see fit and at your own risk.

Any trademarks, service marks, product names, or named features are assumed to be the property of their respective owners. They are used only for reference. Unless specifically stated otherwise, use of such terms implies no endorsement.

Sharing this Document

The bottom line is that you shouldn't.

More specifically, you shouldn't make copies and give them to others.

Loan your copy as you see fit. (Back it up, of course!) However, making an additional copy to *give* to someone else is a no-no. (The rule is pretty simple: if you *loan* the book, they have access to it, and you shouldn't, until they return it. If both you and your friend can use the book at the same time, then you've made a *copy,* and that's the part that's wrong.) That goes for uploading a copy to an electronic bulletin board, website, file sharing or similar type of service.

The information in this document is copyrighted. That means that giving copies to others is actually *illegal*. But more important than that, it's simply wrong.

Instead, if you think it's valuable enough to share, encourage your friends who need this book to buy a copy of their own. Or, heck, buy one as a gift for them.

Remember, it's the sale of valuable information in books like this one that makes Ask Leo! possible. It's pretty simple, really; if enough people disregard that, there'd be no more books, and eventually no more *Ask Leo!*

More *Ask Leo!* Books

If you found this book helpful, check out my growing library of books at
https://store.askleo.com.

Use the coupon code BOOKOWNER when you purchase the PDF download version from The
Ask Leo! Store at check-out, and get *20% off* the regular price.

*The Ask Leo! Guide to Staying Safe on the Internet -
Expanded Edition*

You can use the internet safely!

In this book I cover the things you must do, the software
you must run and the concepts you need to be aware of –
to keep your computer, your data, and yourself safe as you
use the internet.

It's really not that hard, and once things are in place it's
not even that time consuming.

But it is necessary.

Five major areas are covered to keep you safe:

- Never lose precious files, emails or data again: protect your data.
- Reduce the chances of malware ever impacting you dramatically, and recover
  quickly and easily if it ever does: protect your computer.
- Travel worry-free with your laptop and its data protected, as well as securing your
  internet access wherever you may be: protect your laptop.
- Prevent account hacks and how to recover quickly when they happen through no
  fault of your own: protect your online world.
- Learn what we mean by common sense and never fall for scams and scammers
  again: protect yourself.

Yes, you can use the internet with confidence and peace of mind.

The Ask Leo! Guide to Routine Maintenance

The *Ask Leo! Guide to Routine Maintenance* is all about helping you:

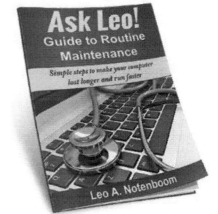

- Keep your computer running longer. There are simple steps you can take, today, to lengthen the useful lifespan of your existing Windows computer.

- Avoid spending money you don't need to spend. By paying attention to some basic maintenance, you can delay unnecessary and often costly upgrades, replacements, and expansions you might not need.

- Speed up your computer. There are things to do, and things to avoid doing, that can keep your computer running as fast as it possibly can, for as long as It possibly can.

- Free up space. Is your disk filling up? There's a good chance that a bunch of it is stuff you don't need. Learn how to identify what to keep and what to trash (and what to back up and *then* trash).

⊙

Just Do This: Back Up!

Is this how you feel when faced with thoughts of backing up?

"I was immediately so overwhelmed that I gave up."

– An *Ask Leo!* reader

If that sounds too true, then *Just Do This: Back Up* is for you.

Backing up doesn't have to be hard to do. Honest. Making copies of everything important is about as simple as it can be.

The problem is that there are so many options. Each option requires a decision. Each decision requires a choice. Each choice is an opportunity for uncertainty and confusion.

Instead of giving option after confusing option, *Just Do This: Back Up* outlines a step-by-step arrangement for backing up your desktop or laptop PC that just works. Follow these instructions, watch the videos included with the book, and you'll be backed up. You'll be protected against everything from hardware failure to malware infestation, and all the minor-to-major inconveniences in between.

Check out these titles and more at <u>The Ask Leo! Store</u>[8].

---

[8] <u>https://askleo.com/shop</u>

33364124R00055

Made in the USA
San Bernardino, CA
22 April 2019